HISTORY HUNTERS

ANCIENT CHINA

Dig Up the Secrets of the Dead

Louise Spilsbury

raintree

a Capstone company — publishers for children

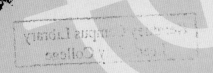

Raintree is an imprint of Capstone Global Library Limited, a company incorporated in England and Wales having its registered office at 264 Banbury Road, Oxford OX2 7DY – Registered company number: 6695582

www.raintree.co.uk
myorders@raintree.co.uk

Produced for Raintree by Calcium
Edited by Sarah Eason and Jennifer Sanderson
Designed by Paul Myerscough
Picture research by Rachel Blount
Consultant: John Malam
Production by Paul Myerscough
Originated by Calcium Creative Limited © 2016
Printed and bound in China

ISBN 978 1 4747 2682 5 (hardback)
20 19 18 17 16
10 9 8 7 6 5 4 3 2 1

ISBN 978 1 4747 2688 7 (paperback)
21 20 19 18 17
10 9 8 7 6 5 4 3 2 1

British Library Cataloguing in Publication Data
A full catalogue record for this book is available from the British Library.

Acknowledgements
We would like to thank the following for permission to reproduce photographs: Corbis p. 11 (Keren Su); Shutterstock pp. 1 (Meaofoto), 4 (Asharkyu), 5 (Hung Chung Chih), 6 (cl2004lhy), 7 (Hecke61), 8 (Hung Chung Chih), 9 (John Leung), 10 (Andrea Paggiaro), 13 (Philip Lange), 15 (Meaofoto), 16 (Hung Chung Chih), 17 (Kalapangha), 19 top (Rudra Narayan Mitra), 19 bottom (TonyV3112), 22 (Javarman), 23 (Tutti Frutti), 24 (Spaceport9), 25 (Zens), 27 (Noppharat46), 28 (Sunxuejun), 29 (Captain Yeo); Wikimedia Commons pp. 12 (Daderot, George Walter Vincent Smith Art Museum), 14 (Hua Shou), 20 (Gary L. Todd, Ph.D., Professor of History, Sias International University, Xinzheng, China), 21 (Shizhao), 26.

Cover photograph reproduced with permission of: Shutterstock: Hung Chung Chih.

CONTENTS

Throughout the book you will find Deadly
Secrets boxes that show an historical object.
Use the clues and the hint in these boxes to
figure out what the object is or what it was
used for. Then check out the Answer box at the
bottom of the page to see if you are right.

ANCIENT CHINA

Ancient China was one of the most incredible **civilizations** in history. Its early rulers were kings who belonged to powerful **dynasties**. Dynasties are families that rule a country for a long time.

The Warring States period (475–221 BC) came after the first three dynasties. This period lasted about 250 years, when the region was divided between many small states. These states constantly fought each other. The Warring States period ended in 221 BC, when the Qin kingdom defeated all the others. The ruler of the Qin kingdom became the first emperor of the newly united China.

The ancient Chinese centred their civilization around the mighty Yellow River.

Harsh and hated

Emperor Qin made new laws. He organized the country into districts. Officials ran these districts. Qin encouraged science and invention. He built roads and canals. He also set up systems of writing, weights and measures. However, his rule was harsh. People hated him because he forced them to pay high **taxes** to fund his building projects. The Qin dynasty lasted just 15 years. The Han dynasty followed from 206 BC to AD 220. It encouraged education, art and science and helped to make China the most advanced civilization the world had ever seen.

Secrets of the Dead

China's first dynasties

- Xia (2070–1600 BC): This was the first family to pass power from father to son, creating a dynasty. Its first king was Yu. He invented channels to bring water to farm fields.
- Shang (1600–1046 BC): In this dynasty, people made glazed pottery and used a potter's wheel. They created objects from **bronze** and made beautiful stone carvings. The last Shang king made his people pay for a huge palace.
- Zhou (1046–256 BC): The Zhou leaders told everyone that their right to rule came from heaven. They said it was a sin to disobey the leaders. Drought, famine, floods and earthquakes were signs that a ruler had lost his right to rule.

Emperor Qin Shi Huang ruled from 221 BC until his death in 210 BC. The word Qin is pronounced "chin". This is how the country of China got its name.

DIGGING UP THE PAST

Secrets to the way ancient Chinese people lived, what they looked like and what tools they used lie under the ground.

When people throw away objects or accidentally lose them, soil gradually buries them. Some objects are buried on purpose. Wood and other materials rot away. However, things such as **clay**, bronze pots and weapons can remain underground for thousands of years. **Archaeologists** have dug up many **artefacts** in China. One of the most famous is an army of life-sized soldiers, horses and chariots made from pottery. It is called the Terracotta Army.

DEADLy Secrets

This is the bronze mechanism from an ancient Chinese crossbow. The wooden parts have rotted away. Written records suggest that mechanically triggered crossbows were installed around Emperor Qin's **tomb** when it was built. Why do you think that was?

Hint: Qin did not want to be disturbed after he died.

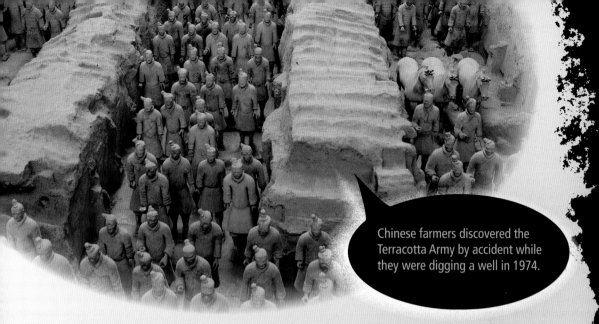

Chinese farmers discovered the Terracotta Army by accident while they were digging a well in 1974.

Preparations for the afterlife

The ancient Chinese believed in an **afterlife**. They buried items with the dead for their next life. Emperor Qin had clay reproductions of his army made to protect him in his next life. Qin's tomb is under a hill near the Terracotta Army. The tomb has not yet been opened because an ancient story says it is surrounded by an underground moat of poisonous mercury. Some archaeologists fear it may be too dangerous to explore his tomb.

Secrets of the Dead

Amazing facts about the Terracotta Army

- It took 700,000 workers about 38 years to build the Terracotta Army more than 2,200 years ago.
- There are around 8,000 life-sized pottery figures in three huge pits.
- Each warrior is unique. Each has individual clothing, hair and facial features. It is thought that they were probably based on real soldiers who served in the emperor's army.
- The Army includes archers, foot soldiers, officers, chariots and hundreds of horses.

Answer: The crossbows were set to shoot any intruders who tried to enter the tomb where Emperor Qin's body lies. Many treasures are rumoured to be buried with Qin.

DEADLY WEAPONS AND
GIANT WALLS

Chinese kingdoms fought each other. After Emperor Qin united the country, the Chinese feared attack of a different kind. They developed deadly weapons and amazing structures to protect their lands from outsiders.

Emperor Qin began building a giant wall along the northern border of the country. He forced hundreds of thousands of soldiers, prisoners of war and ordinary people to work on it. Other emperors made the wall longer over hundreds of years, until the Great Wall of China became one of the longest and biggest ancient structures in the world.

The Great Wall is made up of many different walls that join together and wind across the Chinese countryside.

Amazing facts about the Great Wall of China

- Sticky rice soup was mixed with lime to make a super-strong mortar that stuck bricks and stones together along the Great Wall.
- The high towers along the wall were used as watchtowers and signal towers. The lower levels contained rooms for soldiers. Fires could be built on top to send signals.
- There were passes along the Great Wall that had heavily protected gates where merchants and other people could get in and out.
- The height of the Great Wall ranges from 5 to 14 metres (16 to 46 feet).
- By the 1500s, more than 2,000 years after it was begun, the Great Wall stretched for 8,850 kilometres (5,500 miles).

Weapons of war

Ancient Chinese weapons helped the emperors to beat their enemies and become very powerful. Soldiers chased and attacked enemies in horse-drawn war chariots. They used large bows and arrows. They also had spears with steel tips, and doubled-edged swords made from bronze. Skilled soldiers could launch 10 bolts every 15 seconds from their crossbows. Ancient Chinese soldiers also used kites. They sent signals to their friends on kites and they attached bells and flutes that howled in the wind to scare their enemies.

Deadly weapons like these gave the ancient Chinese the power to fight wars.

INCREDIBLE INVENTIONS

The ancient Chinese came up with many amazing inventions.

In the AD 800s, chemists trying to create a potion to make the emperor **immortal** discovered that a certain mixture of substances exploded when heated. They had invented gunpowder by accident.

Portable paper

People used to write on bones, wood and bamboo. These were so bulky and heavy that they often had to be carried in wheelbarrows (another Chinese invention). In AD 105, an official named Ts'ai Lun invented paper. Paper was ideal for writing on. It is light so it was easy to store and carry. Officials began to use paper to spread laws and information throughout China.

DEADly Secrets

This gadget was invented in the Warring States period in ancient China. The spoon-shaped object is a piece of lodestone (magnetic iron **ore**) that sits on a bronze plate. The handle of the ladle points south. What do you think this is?

Hint: People could use it to work out which way to travel.

Earthquake detector

The first machine for detecting earthquakes was invented in ancient China in AD 132. This bronze pot had eight holes covered by dragon heads. If an earthquake shook the ground even a little, a bronze ball rolled out of the head that pointed in the direction of the centre of the earthquake.

When a ball fell out of a dragon's mouth, it rolled into a metal toad's mouth. This made a sound to tell people an earthquake had happened.

Secrets of the Dead

How paper was made in ancient China

- Bits of old rope, rags, bamboo fibres and bark were boiled with wood ash or lime.
- When these fibres were soft, they were beaten into a mushy pulp.
- An extract from birch tree leaves was added to strengthen the pulp. It also made the pulp smooth.
- This mixture was filtered through a flat strainer. The strainer was made of woven cloth stretched in a four-sided bamboo frame.
- The damp fibres left flat on the strainer were dried to form a sheet of paper.

Answer: It did not work brilliantly well but this is what the world's first **compass** looked like. It was made in the 200s BC. The Chinese characters on the metal plate show different directions of north, north-east, east and so on.

ANCIENT BELIEFS AND SCARY SACRIFICES

In ancient China, people believed in many different gods. Some gods were representations of the weather or natural forces. There was a god of lightning and a god of the Moon. Large rivers and mountains also had their own gods.

The Chinese believed that when people died, they joined the gods in the spirit world. When people died, they were buried with objects they would need in the spirit world. Poor people were buried with simple pots. An important person was buried with objects made from a precious green stone called jade. They believed that jade had magical powers and could protect the dead from bad spirits and preserve the body. Some powerful people were buried in whole suits made of jade.

Jade burial suits like this were made from more than 2,000 plates of jade. Gold, silver or copper wire was used to sew the plates together around the body.

The Three Ways

Some Chinese gods came from three belief systems that became popular after the Zhou dynasty (see page 5). In **Taoism**, there are hundred of gods. Taoists use **meditation** and fortune telling. They chant religious texts in their worship. Followers of **Confucianism** use the teachings of a man named Confucius. Confucius was born in 551 BC. He taught that rulers must be fair and that ordinary people need to obey rulers. By the end of the Han dynasty (206 BC – AD 220), **Buddhism** reached China. Buddhists believe in the teachings of the Buddha. They believe that when people die, they are reborn. For Buddhists, rebirth ends only after someone lives a "proper" life.

Confucius taught people to live in peace by carrying out their different duties and respecting others.

Secrets of the Dead

How the ancient Chinese buried their dead

During the Qin dynasty, when the Terracotta Army was built, pottery figures were buried in tombs. Before 221 BC, human sacrifices also took place. When an emperor or prince died, people who were close to him were buried in the same chamber. This meant they could be with him in the afterlife. Servants and guards were buried in a chamber nearby. Evidence from skeletons that archaeologists have found in tombs suggests that these people were alive when they were buried!

TRADITIONAL
CHINESE
MEDICINE

During the early dynasties, people believed that demons or curses caused illnesses. Cures included chanting spells and eating what the Chinese thought were crushed dragon bones. They were actually fossilized animal bones.

By the Han dynasty (206 BC – AD 220), Chinese healers used a variety of treatments. They made herbal medicines from plant parts and tree bark. They made healing teas from plants or dried parts of animals, such as scorpions and insects.

Ancient cures

The ancient Chinese also treated patients by placing hot cups on the body to draw blood to the surface. This is known as cupping. **Acupuncture** is an ancient Chinese medicine in which needles are inserted into the body. Acupuncture and cupping are still used today.

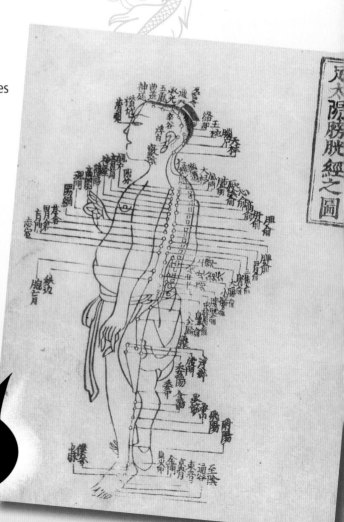

This drawing shows the main points of the body as used by ancient Chinese acupuncturists.

How acupuncture works

Acupuncture has been used for more than 2,000 years. In ancient China, using acupuncture needles was a special skill passed down from father to son. A healer put thin needles into a patient's body for about 30 minutes to reduce pain and cure illness. The needles were inserted at points along 12 lines, called meridians. Each meridian was linked to a different organ of the body. Chinese healers believed that the life force of the body flowed along these lines. Today, acupuncture is used to treat back pain, toothache and headaches, and to stop people feeling ill.

Yin and yang

Yin and yang was the most important theory in traditional Chinese medicine. Chinese healers believed that the reason people became ill was because two forces, called yin and yang, were out of balance. Things that could knock them out of balance included eating rotten or unhealthy food, not exercising or keeping clean and stress. Doctors used traditional medicines to cure people. Governments built sewage systems and taught people to boil drinking water. To keep healthy, the ancient Chinese were also taught to wash their hands before eating.

The yin yang **symbol** is at the centre of this metal disc. It stands for the two sides of things that complement each other.

CLEVER FARMERS AND IRON TOOLS

Most people in ancient China were farmers. They worked on land owned by a king or lord. In the warm, wet southern regions, people grew rice. In the cooler, drier north, they grew mainly cereal plants, such as wheat and millet.

Other crops included tea, soya beans and vegetables. Farmers may have owned dogs, chickens, pigs and sometimes oxen. However, they did most of their work by hand, using stone, wood and iron tools.

Secrets of the Dead

A farmer's duties

Most farmers were very poor and worked hard day and night. They still had to leave their farm and work for the government for about one month every year. They worked for the army or helped to build canals, city walls and palaces. Farmers also had to give their lord part of their crops as a tax to the government and the emperor.

These beautiful ancient rice terraces, called the Dragon's Backbone, are still in use in southern China.

Growing rice

Rice grows only in water so farmers grew it in marshes. These were fields called paddy fields that they flooded with water. Growing rice was back-breaking work because young rice plants had to be pushed into the mud by hand, one by one. Crops were also grown on terraces. Terraces were like giant steps cut into hills and mountains. Digging terraces created more land for farming. Terraces captured the rain that would otherwise run down the slope.

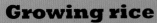

DEADly Secrets

The ancient Chinese were the first to invent a V-shaped iron plough to dig the soil. By the Han dynasty, farmers were using iron ploughs with an iron tip. This helped a second, larger iron board to turn the soil. Oxen pulled the plough. Why do you think the iron plough was so important?

Hint: Only about one-tenth of China's land is suitable for growing crops and there were a lot of mouths to feed in ancient China.

Answer: The plough made neat rows of furrows (long, narrow trenches for planting seeds and young plants) quickly and efficiently. This allowed farmers to grow more food for the country's large and growing population.

SUCCESSFUL TRADE AND SKILLED WORKERS

While the majority of people in ancient China worked on the land, there were other jobs, too. There were officials, craftsmen and artists, and merchants and tradesmen.

Officials made rules and laws. Craftsmen and artists created useful items or luxurious ones such as decorative, **lacquered** wooden boxes. Merchants and tradesmen sold goods. The ancient Chinese built roads and canals to transport goods for sale within the country. Chinese merchants carried goods to the rest of Asia and beyond, in boats called junks. They also used camels or carts to travel along a route known as the Silk Road.

Secrets of the Dead

What was the Silk Road?

The Silk Road was a 6,437-kilometre (4,000 mile) route through deserts and mountain ranges that reached from China to the Mediterranean. It was called the Silk Road because the main product transported along it was silk cloth. Chinese merchants also **exported** tea, salt, sugar, porcelain and spices. On their return journey, they brought back cotton, ivory, wool, gold and silver to sell in China. Merchants and tradesmen travelled in groups with guards because their cargo was very valuable.

The Silk Road passed through remote and often dry, harsh landscapes.

DEADly Secrets

Some of the earliest coins in the world come from ancient China. During the Qin dynasty in the 300s BC, the whole empire started to use the same type of coin for trade. Why do you think the coins have holes in them?

Hint: There were no banks in ancient China. •••••

Skilled craftsmen

The ancient Chinese were skilled at many crafts. They were the first people to make cast iron, which they did in the 400s BC. Metalworkers heated iron ore in an oven until it was molten. Then they shaped it into moulds to make different objects. Lacquer is an art in which workers apply thin layers of lacquer (a varnish made from the sap of the lacquer tree) to wood or bamboo. They would often add red or black colouring to it first. When the lacquer dries, it gives objects a hard, glossy coating.

Answer: Ancient Chinese coins had holes in the middle so people could store lots of them together on long pieces of string.

CROWDED CITIES AND GRAND PALACES

Some cities in ancient China, such as Chang'an (Xi'an), were huge. Hundreds of thousands of people lived in them. The cities had high walls with gates. The gates were locked at night so no one could leave or enter the cities.

Kings and emperors lived within the city walls in palaces. Moats and walls surrounded the palaces to keep the rulers safe. The palaces had courtyards that were open to the sky. Palace buildings were made from earth and wood.

Some palaces were huge. Weiyang Palace was the largest palace ever built in the world. It covered almost 5 square kilometres (1.9 square miles).

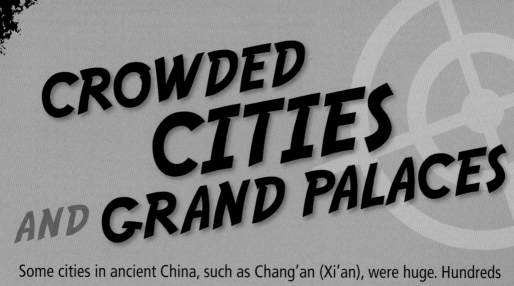

Ancient Chinese palaces

Royal palaces had buildings where the ruler, his family and servants lived. They also had halls for ceremonies and for rulers to meet with their ministers. They had temples, towers and gardens, too. Rooms were filled with luxury objects such as bronze candlesticks and china vases. Some palaces had large statues of lions outside their doors. Real lions were brought along the Silk Road and given as pets to the emperor. They were believed to have magical powers of protection.

DEADly Secrets

This bronze statue of a female servant is covered with gold. It was found in a tomb alongside about 3,000 other objects made of bronze, gold, silver, jade, pottery, lacquer and silk. It shows the kind of luxury that was found in ancient Chinese palaces. This object was also very useful. What do you think it was?

Hint: The servant is holding up an object designed to help a princess to see at night.

Home sweet home?

Compared with palaces, ordinary people's homes were very basic. Up to three **generations** of the same family lived in small mud houses with a thatched roof. The house often consisted of only one room. There was little furniture, possibly just wooden benches to sit on, and a pit in the ground in the middle of the house for a fire. The fire was used for cooking and to keep people warm.

Answer: The servant is holding an oil lamp. The sliding door allowed people to adjust the direction and brightness of the light and stopped the smoke escaping into a room.

HEALTHY FOOD
AND STOLEN FISH

In ancient China, people ate a healthy diet. In the south, people ate a lot of rice cooked in boiling water. In northern China, they ate millet boiled into a kind of porridge.

Archaeologists have also discovered a 4,000-year-old bowl of long, thin noodles. Noodles were made from millet and later rice and wheat, too. Dishes were often flavoured with the root from the ginger plant. People drank water, tea and wine made from rice.

DEADly Secrets

Sticks like these have been used since the Zhou dynasty. During the Zhou dynsasty, emperors sent hunters into central China to get tusks from the elephants that roamed there. They used the tusks to make special versions of these sticks. What are they?

Hint: People found it tricky to use spoons to dip vegetables in their soup.

This modern-day fisherman uses cormorants to catch fish just like the ancient Chinese did.

Birds at work

Poor people ate their rice and millet with a lot of vegetables. Vegetables were considered important for good health. They sometimes ate fish, too. On China's coast and rivers, people trained cormorants to catch fish, as they do today. They put rings or cords around the birds' throats to stop them swallowing the fish so the fisherman can take the catch instead. When the fisherman takes the cormorant's catch, he gives the bird some fish as a reward so it will dive again.

Secrets of the Dead

Food fit for an emperor

Emperors and their families ate a wide variety of meat, including horse, beef, pork, mutton and deer, as well as vegetables.

- Chefs were so important in the Shang dynasty (1600–1046 BC) that one was even chosen to be a government minister.
- In the Zhou dynasty (1046–256 BC), 2,000 people prepared meals for the emperor and his family.
- Many new **delicacies** came to China along the Silk Road, such as oranges from central Asia.
- At feasts and festivals, they also ate roasted duck, pheasant, wild boar and bear paw.

Answer: They are chopsticks, invented to grip pieces of vegetable. In ancient China, people dipped vegetables in soup.

FAMILIES: RESPECT AND RITUALS

In ancient China, family included not only living relatives but dead ones, too! The father was the ruler of the house. His wife and children had to obey everything he said. After relatives died, the family continued to show its respect to them.

The ancient Chinese believed that their relatives could speak to the gods in the afterlife. If a person kept his or her **ancestors** happy, the ancestors would ask the gods to bring the family good luck. If the ancestors were not properly worshipped, they could bring bad luck.

Boys and girls

In ancient China, boys were treated as if they were more important than girls. Boys from rich families went to school. They learnt writing, religious **rituals**, archery and mathematics so they could get jobs in government, the army or as priests. Girls from rich families had to stay at home. They were taught things like spinning, weaving and sewing. Children in poor families worked with their parents. They helped out at home and on the family farm.

Children always had to respect, obey and, sometimes, worship their parents, even after they became adults themselves.

Ancient Chinese ancestor worship

- In the Shang dynasty (1600–1046 BC), animals and, sometimes, humans, were sacrificed to honour dead kings. People also brought food and drink in bronze cups and bowls as offerings to dead rulers.
- Ordinary families set up a home **altar**. There they kept tablets of stone to represent dead relatives. They lit **incense** (a substance that creates a sweet smell when burnt) and left food and drink offerings at the altar. They also prayed, discussed important decisions and held ceremonies there.

DEADly Secrets

This beautiful bronze object was used in ancestor-worship ceremonies. Large numbers of these objects were hit with hammers in particular sequences to make sounds. What do you think it is?

Hint: It was used in ancient Chinese rituals to communicate with dead ancestors.

Answer: It is a bo, or bell. It required great skill to tune these bells to different notes.

SILK ROBES AND ROUGH TUNICS

In ancient China, people could tell how important or rich someone was by their clothes. There were many rules about what should be worn. People could be punished if they wore the wrong colour or type of outfit.

An emperor, his advisors and officials wore long robes. These were made from coloured silks. Silk is made from the cocoons of silkworms. The Chinese were the first to make this luxurious fabric. Emperors also wore different colours to **symbolize** their rule. Zhou dynasty emperors wore red to represent fire. Emperor Qin wore black, which represented water. This suggested that he had put out the fire of the Zhou dynasty and was more powerful!

This portrait of Emperor Qin shows him wearing robes decorated with dragons. The ancient Chinese believed these creatures existed. Emperors wore dragon symbols to show their power.

How the ancient Chinese made silk

The Chinese kept their method for making silk a secret for hundreds of years.
- Hundreds of moths lay around 500 eggs each.
- The **larvae** (or silkworms) that hatch from the eggs are fed mulberry leaves for a month.
- The larvae spin cocoons around themselves when they are ready to turn into moths.
- The cocoons are steamed to kill the moths inside.
- Women carefully unwind the long threads that form the cocoons.
- These threads are spun together to make them thicker.
- Women weave the threads into silk cloth.

It takes a silkworm about three days to make a cocoon using about 900 metres (0.5 mile) of silk. The Chinese used the threads to make beautiful silk garments.

Cloth for the peasants

Poor people wore cheap, hard-wearing clothes. Instead of decorative layers of silk, they wore simple tunics, trousers and padded jackets made from plant fibres such as **hemp**. While the rich wore cloth slippers, poor people often walked barefoot or wore shoes made from straw. One thing the rich and poor had in common was long hair. The ancient Chinese said that because people got their hair from their parents, it was very disrespectful to cut it.

THE POWER OF WRITING

The ancient Chinese began to use writing more than 3,000 years ago. The earliest form of writing used picture symbols.

Emperors used these symbols to have laws and important statements carved into the side of mountains and on stone columns. They were also cut into the surface of jade and bronze ritual objects. The earliest examples of Chinese writing are found on "oracle bones", which emperors used to **divine**, or tell the future. Oracle bones were made from tortoise shells or the shoulder bones of oxen. The Shang emperors used oracle bones before making decisions.

The importance of writing

During later dynasties, the picture symbols changed shape and emperors encouraged people to use a standard system of writing. This system has more than 40,000 signs called characters. Each one has to be written in a certain way and each one must be learnt by heart. Calligraphy, or the art of beautiful handwriting, was the most important art in ancient China. Chinese writing provides us with many clues about ancient China. Using the written word helped China to develop one of the most advanced civilizations in the ancient world.

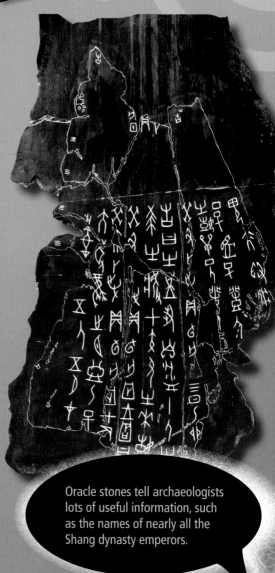

Oracle stones tell archaeologists lots of useful information, such as the names of nearly all the Shang dynasty emperors.

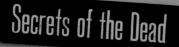

How oracle bones were used

- The emperor told a diviner what question he needed answered. For example: "Will there be enough rain to water the crops this year?"
- The diviner made pits or holes in the surface of the oracle bones.
- He asked the oracle bone the emperor's question.
- He heated the bone until it cracked. If the bone cracked on one side, the answer to the question was yes. If it cracked on the other, the answer was no.
- Finally, the emperor's name, the date, the diviner's name, the answer and the number of cracks were inscribed on the bone.

Calligraphers wrote with brushes dipped in ink. It took them years to learn the thousands of Chinese characters. Calligraphers were highly respected in ancient China.

GLOSSARY

acupuncture treatment in which fine needles are inserted at certain points in the body to stop pain and prevent illness

afterlife life after death, or the idea that there is another world people live in after they die

altar table or surface used for a religious ritual

ancestor relative who has died

archaeologist person who digs up and studies the remains of ancient cultures

artefact object made by a human being that has cultural or religious importance

bronze metal made from a mixture of copper and tin

Buddhism religion based on the teachings of Siddhartha Gautama, known as the Buddha

civilization society, culture and way of life of a particular area

clay fine sandy material

compass device that contains a magnetized pointer that usually shows the direction of north

Confucianism religion based on the teachings of Confucius

delicacy something that is considered rare and desirable to eat

divine use supernatural or magical powers to tell the future

dynasty when one family rules a country for a long time, because after a leader dies their oldest son takes over

export send goods to be sold in another country

generation people in a family born and living during the same time

hemp tall herb mainly grown in Asia

immortal everlasting

incense substance that is burnt to give off a sweet smell

lacquered varnished using the sap of the lacquer tree. The varnish is painted on in thin layers to form a hard shell when dry

larva stage in the life cycle of an insect when it looks like a little worm

meditation thinking or reflecting on religious ideas

ore rock from which metal can be extracted

ritual action or set of actions done over and over again for a special purpose, often connected to a person's religion

symbol something that represents or stands for something else

symbolize represent or stand for something else

Taoism Chinese religion that stresses living simply and in harmony with nature

tax regular amount of money people pay to a government or ruler to do things, such as build roads

tomb building or space above or below the ground where a dead body is kept

FIND OUT MORE

Books

Daily Life in Shang Dynasty China (Daily Life in Ancient Civilizations), Lori Hile (Heinemann, 2015)

Shang Dynasty China (Great Civilisations), Tracey Kelly (Franklin Watts, 2016)

The Great Wall of China (Engineering Wonders), Rebecca Stanborough (Capstone Press, 2016)

The Shang and other Chinese Dynasties (Technology in the Ancient World), Charlie Samuels (Franklin Watts, 2015)

The Shang Dynasty of Ancient China (The History Detective Investigates), Geoffrey Barker (Wayland, 2015)

Websites

Learn more about ancient China, its crafts and rituals and the importance of its writing:
www.ancientchina.co.uk/menu.html

Find extra information about the early dynasties and maps:
www.chaos.umd.edu/history/ancient1.html

This website has lots of details about ancient China:
www.chinaculture.org/gb/en_madeinchina/2005-05/12/content_68567.htm

INDEX